BETH HILLEL LIBRARY

WITHDRAWN

Gift of the

Graduating Class of

1979

COMING OF AGE

YOUR BAR/BAT MITZVAH

*The publication of this book was made possible
by a fund
in memory of
David S. Marx
October 7, 1957 — March 3, 1973*

COMING OF AGE

YOUR BAR/BAT MITZVAH

by BENJAMIN EFRON
and ALVAN D. RUBIN

uahc

Library of Congress Catalog Number: 77-78031

© Copyright 1977

by Union of American Hebrew Congregations
838 Fifth Avenue / New York, N. Y. 10021

PRODUCED IN THE U. S. OF AMERICA

FOREWORD

Coming of Age: Your Bar/Bat Mitzvah represents a total revision of *Your Bar Mitzvah* by the same authors, originally published in 1963.

During the intervening Bar/Bat Mitzvah period of 13 years, almost every UAHC congregation has made provision for the training and ritual experience of both boys and girls, culminating in this most significant Jewish milestone. Hence this new volume, for students ages 11-13, which constitutes a basic introduction to Bar/Bat Mitzvah, its history, ritual, and significance. It is a "must" reading, not only for pupils, but for their parents as well. It adds a measure of understanding which will complement and supplement basic Bar/Bat Mitzvah training. Thousands of young people have already benefited from the earlier volume. Thousands more, we hope, will derive similar guidance and inspiration from the work of Benjamin Efron and Rabbi Alvan Rubin.

We are indebted to many individuals who helped in the preparation of this book — Rabbi Harold Hahn, Rabbi Steven Jacobs, Rabbi Bernard Mehlman, Judith Spiegler Paskind, and Melanie Hahn. As always, we express our gratitude to Ralph Davis, UAHC Director of Publications, and his talented staff and to Arie Haas for his fine illustrations.

We are grateful to the CCAR for permission to use portions of their new prayer book, *Gates of Prayer*.

We hope that you will use this book in your religious schools as a tool with which to further our common goals of Jewish literacy and commitment in the next generation.

Daniel B. Syme
Acting Director
UAHC Department of Education

CONTENTS

By Way of Introduction	1
History of Bar Mitzvah	5
The Torah Reading	13
The Haftarah Portion	26
The Family Celebrates Bar/Bat Mitzvah	31
Glossary	37

by way of INTRODUCTION

Your בַּר/בַּת מִצְוָה, Bar/Bat Mitzvah, is an exciting ceremony to look forward to. Besides being a wonderful occasion for rejoicing on the part of your family and friends, it is also one of the first times in your life when you are an active participant on the בִּימָה (bimah), pulpit, during a synagogue service.

If you started your religious education when you were about six, the chances are you took part in a Torah-reading service shortly after you began school because many Reform and other synagogues have a Consecration ritual for new students around the time of שִׂמְחַת תּוֹרָה (Simchat Torah), Rejoicing of the Torah. At that time of the year, the weekly readings from the Torah reach the end of דְּבָרִים (Devarim), Deuteronomy, the last book of the חוּמָשׁ (Chumash), the Five Books of Moses.

However, we do not stop the Torah readings at that point and wait until the following week to begin again with בְּרֵאשִׁית (Bereshit), Genesis, the first of the books. Instead, we read the last verses of Deuteronomy and immediately continue with the first verses of Genesis, showing that the study of Torah should not be broken off; it should never end. Many rabbis have chosen the time of that Torah reading to bring new children in the synagogue school to the *bimah* for a blessing.

If you took part in such a ceremony, you probably did not understand what it was all about, but you may remember it with a warm feeling. You may have received a miniature Torah scroll or a copy of the Ten Commandments. Perhaps cookies and sweets were served, perhaps your parents kissed you, and, surely, everybody seemed happy.

It will be different at your Bar/Bat Mitzvah. Of course there will be a party of some sort, and everyone will be feeling good. But, there will be a difference. You will know a good deal more about the meaning of your Bar/Bat Mitzvah service. You have no doubt been thinking about it in recent months, not only about what you will be called upon to do at the ceremony, but also about its significance so far as your own view of life is concerned.

You will be getting some help at your religious school to prepare you for the service — reading this booklet may even be part of that program — but many things you learned during your years of Jewish study will now begin to come together in your mind. For instance, you know that you may be called up for an עֲלִיָה *(aliyah)*, "going up," to read or chant from the Torah; certainly, you will

By Way of Introduction

have the honor of chanting the הַפְטָרָה *(haftarah)*, the selected reading from the Prophets. Also, you probably know that now, accepted as an adult in the religious sense, you will be counted in the מִנְיָן *(minyan)*, the number of adults required for a synagogue service. You may also know that not all congregations are ready to count girls as part of a *minyan*, or even to have them read from the Torah during a service. Why some do not, and why Reform and some other synagogues generally do, will be discussed later in this booklet.

Although it is a meaningful part of one's growth to be thought of as a man or woman in the religious sense, no dramatic change, socially or physically, really takes place when you have your Bar/Bat Mitzvah. You will not be fully grown at that time; you will, of course, continue to grow and mature. Things at school will be the same; you will continue attending your junior high school as before. And no great change will take place in your position in the family; you will remain a student and a minor, still dependent upon your parents for food, clothing, shelter, and other forms of support. But so far as your own image and your status in the Jewish community, these do change. Your rights, privileges, and responsibilities as a Jew are different when you become a Bar/Bat Mitzvah, as you will read later on.

In various ways, your years in religious school have helped to prepare you for this big step. You have been studying Hebrew, and you can follow and read the Hebrew portions of worship services. You have learned about many Jewish customs and ceremonies, and you have some knowledge of Jewish history and teachings which will help you participate in your Bar/Bat Mitzvah service.

But you will need some additional training, especially for the service itself. You will have to learn a number of things that you will be called upon to do during the service: to read or chant various בְּרָכוֹת *(berachot)*, blessings, connected with the Torah service; to read or chant your *haftarah* portion; and, in many synagogues, to read or chant at least part of the סִדְרָה *(sidrah)*, Torah portion of the week. There are other matters relating to Bar/Bat Mitzvah that you will need to learn, too, if the experience is to be a truly meaningful one.

That is the purpose of this booklet, to help you prepare for this wonderful occasion and to organize your thoughts about Judaism so that you will appreciate the religious meaning of the ceremony. We want to help make your Bar/Bat Mitzvah an inspiring event in your life, inasmuch as it marks the end of your childhood and puts you on the road to religious adulthood.

History of Bar Mitzvah

Up until the 1920s, the Bar Mitzvah was restricted to males. The custom of marking a boy's thirteenth birthday in a special way is thought by some to have been a kind of initiation into the tribe. However, our Hebrew ancestors did have an initiation-type of rite for boys, which they called בְּרִית מִילָה (*Berit Milah*), circumcision. That ceremony is mentioned often in the תַּנַ"ךְ (*Tanach*), all twenty-four books of our Bible, but nowhere in the *Tanach* can we find a single reference to Bar Mitzvah. As a matter of fact, no one in biblical times, neither Abraham, Isaac, Moses, David, nor the great prophets, had a Bar Mitzvah.

There is nothing in our written records to tell us when the first Bar Mitzvah took place, but we do have a number of clues which suggest that the custom began about 1,800

years ago. Judah ben Tema, a talmudic rabbi of those days, made a statement that is recorded in פִּרְקֵי אָבוֹת (Pirke Avot), Sayings of the Fathers: בֶּן שְׁלשׁ־עֶשְׂרֵה לַמִּצְווֹת (ben shelosh-esreh lamitzvot), "thirteen [is the age] for [the fulfillment of] the commandments." (5:24).

This indicates that Jews of those days were already thinking of thirteen as the age at which we must accept responsibility for the commandments of Judaism.

Still, we have no notion of what, if anything, was done in those years to mark the birthday. The first written record we have of a special Bar Mitzvah ceremony, to celebrate a boy's coming of religious age, is in the thirteenth century. But, by that time, references to Bar Mitzvah seem to indicate that it had already become a widely accepted custom.

It seems reasonable to say, therefore, that it is a fairly old Jewish tradition to set thirteen apart as a milestone religious birthday. The Jewish youngster leaves behind childhood, when his parents were responsible for his religious as well as other needs, and enters religious adulthood, when he himself becomes accountable for carrying out the commandments. At an Orthodox Bar Mitzvah, this idea is expressed in a blessing which the father recites: בָּרוּךְ שֶׁפְּטָרַנִי מֵעָנְשׁוּ שֶׁל זֶה (Baruch shepetarani me'onsho shel zeh), "Blessed be He who has freed me from the [religious] responsibility for this child."

While the concept behind Bar Mitzvah is an old one, specific ways of observing it have been developed only in the last few hundred years. In the time of your great-grandfather, and of his great-grandfather, and his in turn, it was already a long established tradition to mark a boy's

Bar Mitzvah by calling him up to the Torah during the synagogue service immediately after his thirteenth birthday. While the ceremony usually took place at the שַׁבָּת, *Shabbat*, morning service, it has been held on Saturday afternoons and on Mondays and Thursday mornings and on holidays when the Torah was read.

In most communities the boy started wearing a טַלִּית *(talit)*, prayer shawl, at his Bar Mitzvah service. He also began to put on תְּפִילִין *(tefilin)*, phylacteries, for morning prayers at home. *Tefilin* are two black leather boxes fastened to leather straps, containing four portions from the Torah, that are strapped to the forehead and on the left forearm.

In the early days, a festive meal was held in the boy's home after the synagogue service. It tended to be modest; most Jews lived in cramped quarters and most of them, too, were poor. But, with the passage of time, the family meal became more like a party. After all, Bar Mitzvah is a שִׂמְחָה *(simchah)*, a joyful occasion, and the *mitzvot* were looked upon as pleasure-giving, not burdensome. Whoever could afford it wanted to make it as joyous an occasion as possible. Often, in larger Jewish communities, the parents arranged for lavish banquets in public halls. Some Jews became alarmed at this. For instance, in 1595, almost 400 years ago, officials of the Jewish community of Cracow, Poland, placed a communal tax on Bar Mitzvah celebrations in order to keep them from becoming excessive displays of wealth.

People feared that the religious significance of the occasion would be overshadowed by the gala party after the service. Many Jews are still concerned about this, but

Jewish communities no longer have the legal power to dictate what families do in celebration of their children's Bar/Bat Mitzvah. Some congregations do set certain limits or standards for receptions held in the temple. But most of them hope that their religious schools will impress upon the prospective Bar/Bat Mitzvah students and their families that the primary aim of the celebration is to experience religious growth and that the celebration should be in good taste.

Reform Judaism Moves Toward Religious Equality for Women

In the ancient Middle East, as in the rest of the world, women were not given the same rights as men. They were kept in a subordinate position in society. (Women are still treated as second-class citizens in many countries of the Middle East.)

The Hebrews were very much a part of Middle Eastern civilization about 3,500 years ago. They grew up with many of the same values and, in Hebrew society, women were also treated as inferiors. Even Moses, our great teacher who gave us many doctrines about the equality of people, overlooked the rights of women until a practical question arose. When the twelve tribes were preparing to go into Canaan to settle, for example, he instructed them to divide the land by lot among the male heads of families. But the five daughters of Tselofchad, of the tribe of Menasheh, objected. Their father had died and left no son.

"Let not our father's name be lost just because he had no son," they said to Moses. "Give *us* a holding among our father's kinsmen." (Numbers 27:4)

Recognizing that their plea was valid, Moses agreed. He

then added a new law to the statutes which he had been preparing for the Hebrews: "If a man dies without leaving a son, you shall transfer his property to his daughter." (Numbers 27:1-8)

This did not give women equal rights in all matters, but it was a step in that direction. It indicated that the laws of Judaism were not to be considered fixed, as a closed book. It acknowledged that the rules were open to change when new conditions pointed to the need for an adjustment in the statutes and practices of the faith.

There were in fact many changes and adjustments in Jewish law and tradition in times past, but in the area of religious practice, matters did not change much for women. Men had performed the rituals relating to worship practices in ancient times, and they continued to do so even when the Temple in Jerusalem was destroyed and the synagogue became the center of Jewish life. Men led the prayer services and participated in the rites that took place on the *bimah*. Women were permitted to attend the worship service but were assigned to a section of the synagogue that was either screened off or separated by a מְחִיצָה *(mechitzah)*, partition, from the main part of the sanctuary where the men prayed. And, in the main, it was the boys who were taught Hebrew and given religious training, and only they were prepared for Bar Mitzvah.

When the Reform Movement began in the early 1800s in Germany, the reformers, rabbis and congregational leaders who were rebelling against some practices and traditions of old, saw that the position of women in the synagogue needed change. They inaugurated the practice of family seating at prayer services, abolishing the separation between men and women in the synagogue. From the beginning, Reform congregations fostered religious education for girls, and the movement introduced a new religious ceremony, Confirmation, which included girls as well as boys.

The early reformers did not look with favor on the custom of Bar Mitzvah. To them, a boy was nowhere near being a "man" at age thirteen, although hundreds of years ago, when children started to work for a living as early as eight or nine years of age, a boy could be close to doing an adult's job by thirteen. But, in the last 130 years or so, many nations passed compulsory education laws and abolished child labor. Thirteen year olds were no longer workers. They became students, needing more time to grow, both mentally and emotionally.

Another reason why many Reform rabbis objected to Bar Mitzvah was that it was undemocratically limited to boys. This simply continued the old tradition of relegating women to a kind of second-class citizenship in religion. Reform rabbis in North America urged congregations to add the new ceremony of Confirmation that had been introduced by the movement in Germany in 1810. This was for boys and girls together, and it took place a few years after age thirteen, thus giving students more time to inquire into the deeper meanings of Judaism. In time, all Reform congregations adopted Confirmation, and its popularity in American Jewish communities grew to such a point that Conservative and some Orthodox congregations also made it part of the religious studies program for their youth.

For a time, Bar Mitzvah, as a religious custom, declined

in Reform congregations, but Confirmation did not elbow it out of the picture altogether. Bar Mitzvah had become a strong tradition in Jewish life and many families, even though they had joined the Reform movement, wanted it for their sons. Consequently, many rabbis continued the practice, seeing in it an opportunity for a deeply satisfying spiritual event for the boy and his family. But, there still was no worship service ritual for girls until Confirmation at age sixteen.

Then, in the 1920s, rabbis of various Jewish movements began to experiment with a Bat Mitzvah ceremony for girls. It took a while for the Jewish community to adjust to the idea of girls becoming "daughters of the commandment" for they could not accept the idea of their wearing a *talit*, or calling them up to read the Torah, or of having them put on *tefilin*. Orthodox rabbis were and still are against Bat Mitzvah. The custom, however, began to flourish in non-Orthodox congregations because they looked upon the forms and traditions of Judaism as being more flexible. They could experiment more freely, and Bat Mitzvah became a companion ceremony to Bar Mitzvah.

In most Reform congregations, girls who are preparing for Bat Mitzvah are given the same preparations as boys. They are called up for an *aliyah* to read or chant the *berachot* and the Torah and *haftarah* portions. But there is no rule prescribing a single acceptable formula for a Bar/Bat Mitzvah. Reform congregations are autonomous, having the right to choose their own forms of observance, or even to decide not to have Bar/Bat Mitzvah at all. What follows in this manual, therefore, does not attempt to say what you congregation *should* do about Bar/Bat Mitzvah. Rather, it tells what a large number of Reform congregations *are* doing, and why.

THE TORAH READING

There is a good deal of sense in making the Torah reading the high point of the Bar/Bat Mitzvah ceremony. Giving the boy or girl of thirteen an *aliyah* is a concrete way of saying: "You have moved up into a new stage of your growth as a Jew." For it is the Torah, the original teachings of Moses, which he brought to the Israelites in the name of God. Using the Torah as a basis, the great Hebrew prophets and the later rabbis and teachers developed the modern religion of Judaism.

The public reading of the Torah is a very old tradition in Judaism. In reality, Moses began it for he kept a written record of the statutes and doctrines he taught the Israelites in the wilderness. On various occasions he passed on this "book of teachings" to Joshua who also read from it to the

Israelites. After the Hebrews had settled in Canaan, however, the custom of reading from it seemed to die out. Gradually, Hebrew worship became centralized in the Temple at Jerusalem where the sacrifice of animals and products of the soil was the key element of the service. The כֹּהֲנִים (Kohanim), Temple priests, performed the ritual of preparing the sacrificial animal for roasting on the fire of the altar, and often the people ate of the sacrifice afterwards. But, this type of worship did not include regular readings from the "book of teachings."

The practice of reading from the Torah (this word also means teaching) was resumed for a brief time in 621 B.C.E. In that year, a priest of the Temple in Jerusalem found a long-lost and evidently long-forgotten copy of a book Moses had written, known today as Deuteronomy, the fifth book of the Bible. Josiah, king of Judah, gathered the people together and read the book to the whole assembly. Because there were many laws and practices in it that the Hebrews of Judah were not following, Josiah made a promise to God to observe all the commandments of the covenant that were contained in the book. And the people vowed with him to uphold the covenant, as their ancestors had done at Sinai. (II Kings 23:1-3)

We have little direct evidence that the Torah was read with any regularity after Josiah's covenant ceremony. However, about a generation later, when the Temple was destroyed by the Babylonians, the Hebrews were taken into exile in Babylon and, there, the people read and seriously studied the Torah and the writings of great prophets.

Another, and even more important, reading of the

THE TORAH READING

Torah took place in 444 B.C.E. This was the year that Ezra, a great scribe and teacher in Babylon, returned to Jerusalem. When he came to Zion (a traditional name used to refer to Jerusalem) with a large number of followers, he found that the Jews of Jerusalem knew next to nothing about the Five Books of Moses as they had been compiled in Babylon. It troubled Ezra that the Jerusalem Hebrews were breaking many of the laws and commandments contained in the sacred scriptures. Telling us graphically how the life of the Judeans caused him great grief and torment, Ezra wrote: "I rent my garment and my mantle and plucked off the hair of my head and of my beard and sat down appalled." (Ezra 9:3)

He was not the kind of man to run away from a difficult challenge. Ezra sent out a call and "all the people gathered themselves together as one person into the broad place that was before the water gate" in Jerusalem. The day happened to be the first day of the seventh month of the Hebrew calendar, which is today called ראש הַשָּׁנָה *(Rosh Hashanah)*, the New Year. Ezra stood up on a wooden platform so that all would be able to see and hear him, and he began to read aloud from the Torah he had brought from Babylon. Some of his followers helped him with the reading. They stood in different places, saying the words carefully and distinctly. "They gave the sense and caused the people to understand the reading." (Nehemiah 8:2-8)

This particular Torah reading made a very great impression on the Jews of ancient Judea. In time, it led to the regular practice of reading a portion from the Torah at various prayer services.

Ezra's reading was done mainly for the purpose of

educating the people so they would know and understand the sacred text. He could not depend on others to teach Torah to the people for, in his time, Jerusalem did not have many people who knew the Torah well, nor were there schools in which to learn it. In those days, no religion had established schools for teaching the holy books to the people at large. Such study was reserved for priests of various cult temples.

What Ezra impressed upon the Jews was that the knowledge of Torah was a basic requirement for all the people. Study was a commandment and education an obligation. The Jews took this lesson to heart. They read the Torah, not only at Shabbat services, but also during morning services on Mondays, Thursdays, and other occasions as well. The well-known Jewish tradition of study developed from this emphasis on learning Torah, which has resulted in producing so many scholars among our people. Your own study in preparation for your Bar/Bat Mizvah is in keeping with this ancient tradition.

Over the years, the reading of the Torah evolved into a sacred ritual of the synagogue service. It became a way of showing the Jewish people's appreciation for God's gift of

THE TORAH READING

Torah. The scriptural reading was considered so important by the rabbis of old that they incorporated it into the order of the worship service. It was to be done even if the whole congregation consisted of scholars who knew the Torah well.

Thus, your *aliyah* during the service at which you will become a Bar/Bat Mitzvah is part of an old and meaningful ceremony. As you study the portion you will read on that day, you will be concentrating on only one small part of Torah, but you will be getting a taste of the beauty and dignity of Holy Scriptures. In addition, you will be helping the congregation, as you will see in the next section, to express the age-old gratitude of our people for the Torah.

Your Part in the Torah-Reading Service

What you actually do during the service depends very much upon the congregation of which you are a member. You may be given the opportunity to conduct part of the Shabbat service, or you may be called upon to read from the סֵפֶר תּוֹרָה *(Sefer Torah)*, Scroll of the Torah, or perhaps a portion from the נְבִיאִים *(Neviim)*, Prophets. Most synagogues include all three of these honors.

While Reform congregations may differ in the practices they observe, they generally follow the Torah-reading ritual given in the *Union Prayer Book*, published many years ago, or in *Gates of Prayer*, published in 1975. There is little difference between the two insofar as the Torah-reading section of the service is concerned.

The Torah service begins with the reading of selected parts of a psalm, or of other poetic passages that suggest greatness of God, stressing especially His gift of Torah to the people of Israel; Jews have always felt grateful for receiving the Torah at Mount Sinai. After the recitation of these praises, the congregtion rises for the opening of the אֲרוֹן הַקֹּדֶשׁ (Aron Hakodesh), the Holy Ark.

Words of praise and thankfulness for the Torah are then read as reminders of the Torah's part in binding the people Israel to God. The following are examples of such statements:

Let us declare the greatness of our God and give honor to the Torah.	הָבוּ גֹדֶל לֵאלֹהֵינוּ וּתְנוּ כָבוֹד לַתּוֹרָה.
Praised be the One who in His holiness has given the Torah to His people Israel.	בָּרוּךְ שֶׁנָּתַן תּוֹרָה לְעַמּוֹ יִשְׂרָאֵל בִּקְדֻשָּׁתוֹ.
O, house of Jacob, come, let us walk by the light of the Lord.	בֵּית יַעֲקֹב לְכוּ וְנֵלְכָה בְּאוֹר יְהוָה.

Passages such as these are included so as to recall the way our ancestors stood at the foot of Mount Sinai and, when Moses read the Commandments to them, they declared: נַעֲשֶׂה וְנִשְׁמַע (Naaseh venishma), "We will do and obey." Thus, our ancestors pledged themselves to live according to the Covenant of Sinai and, in every generation since then, Jews have repeated that pledge. With these utterances at the start of the Torah-reading service, the congregants are reminded that Jews have a duty to live their lives with attention to the teachings of Torah.

The rabbis included such readings to put the congrega-

THE TORAH READING

tion into the proper mood for listening to what they felt was the word of God. The Torah scroll is taken from the Ark. Its beautiful coverings are reverently removed. It is placed on the reading lectern and unrolled to the *sidrah* for that service. The congregation, seated, awaits the start of the reading.

Practice varies in regard to the number of people who are called up for the Torah reading. In some congregations it is the custom to honor a few members of the Bar/Bat Mitzvah's family by calling them to the Torah. In others, only the Bar/Bat Mitzvah is called. But, no matter how many or few, one of those surely to be honored on your coming-of-age day will be you, yourself.

Whoever is given an *aliyah* recites the traditional *berachot* before the reading. (If your congregation follows the ancient custom of chanting the *berachot* and the *sidrah*, then you will be taught the special melody that is used.) The *berachot* that precede the reading of the Torah are as follows:

Praise the Lord to whom all praise is due.	בָּרְכוּ אֶת יְיָ הַמְבֹרָךְ.
Praised be the Lord to whom our praise is due, now and forever.	בָּרוּךְ יְיָ הַמְבֹרָךְ לְעוֹלָם וָעֶד.
Blessed is the Lord our God, Ruler of the Universe, who has chosen us from all peoples by giving us His Torah.	בָּרוּךְ אַתָּה יְיָ אֱלֹהֵינוּ מֶלֶךְ הָעוֹלָם אֲשֶׁר בָּחַר בָּנוּ מִכָּל הָעַמִּים וְנָתַן לָנוּ אֶת תּוֹרָתוֹ.
Blessed is the Lord, Giver of the Torah.	בָּרוּךְ אַתָּה יְיָ נוֹתֵן הַתּוֹרָה.

When you pronounce these blessings, you are voicing our people's deep feeling of gratitude for being chosen to receive the Torah from God. Its ideas and teachings are available to all peoples today; it has been translated into every living language. Some of its concepts were adopted by other peoples years ago, but when its commandments were given at Sinai and elaborated upon by Moses, during the forty years of wandering in the wilderness, the Hebrews accepted the Torah in its entirety. They made its doctrine of the one God their basic law, and the ethical ideas of the teaching their guide to life. For many long centuries they held fast to the concept that the worship of God required ethical conduct as well as prayer and ritual, while the rest of the world's people clung to pagan myths and practices. These thoughts are embedded in the praises that are expressed when Jews turn to the reading of the weekly portion at a Shabbat service.

In a large number of congregations the Bar/Bat Mitzvah reads or chants the *sidrah*, while those who are given an *aliyah* say only the *berachot* that precede and follow the reading. It will be very important, therefore, for you to learn to read the Hebrew as written in the Torah scroll. In preparation for your coming-of-age, you will have time to study from the *Sefer Torah* itself, and you will be given additional information about it.

You will note that the writing in the Torah scroll is different from the printed Hebrew to which you are accustomed. *Sefer Torah* Hebrew is an ancient, hand-lettered form of Hebrew without נְקוּדוֹת *(nekudot)*, vowel points or punctuation marks, and without נְגִינוֹת *(neginot)*, signs for the chant. These symbols are found above or below the letters of the words in most copies of

THE TORAH READING

the *Tanach*. In earliest times, Hebrew was written without these vowels or marks; so the original books of the Bible were hand lettered and contained none of them. Because the Torah is sacred to us, the scribes in each generation were careful to make each copy exactly like the original. The writing in the Torah scroll of today, therefore, resembles the ancient script.

For a long time, when Hebrew was the official and national language of the Jews, our people had no trouble in reading the Hebrew script of the *Sefer Torah*. But, when Hebrew ceased to be the mother tongue, only learned Jews could be sure that they were reading and pronouncing the words of Holy Scriptures correctly.

Without vowels, one could pronounce the same Hebrew word a number of ways, each one of them having a different meaning. For instance, the word מטה without vowels can be read in at least five different ways: as מִטָה *(mitah)*, bed, or מַטֶה *(mateh)*, stick, or מַטָה *(matah)*, down, or מֻטֶה *(muteh)*, injustice, or מֻטָה *(mutah)*, outspreading. People learned in Hebrew would know which of these words to choose, even without the vowels, for they would understand the sense of the rest of the sentence. But, when Hebrew was no longer familiar to the people, the average person found it difficult to read and understand the Hebrew of the *Sefer Torah*.

Centuries ago, therefore, a number of scholars began to make notations in the margins and above and below the letters. This ensured the correct reading of words and phrases that might be confusing to less informed readers. More and more such notations were made, until finally an important school of scholars organized a system of vowel points to guide the reader to the proper pronunciation of each word. They also devised musical signs to give each phrase its traditional melody. By the ninth and tenth centuries, this group of scholars, whom we call the Masoretes, had developed all the signs, marks, and notes that we see in printed Hebrew Bibles today. This is called the Masoretic Text, a sample of which is shown below:

בְּרֵאשִׁ֖ית בָּרָ֣א אֱלֹהִ֑ים אֵ֥ת הַשָּׁמַ֖יִם וְאֵ֥ת הָאָֽרֶץ׃ וְהָאָ֗רֶץ 1
הָיְתָ֥ה תֹ֨הוּ֙ וָבֹ֔הוּ וְחֹ֖שֶׁךְ עַל־פְּנֵ֣י תְה֑וֹם וְר֣וּחַ אֱלֹהִ֔ים
מְרַחֶ֖פֶת עַל־פְּנֵ֥י הַמָּֽיִם׃ וַיֹּ֥אמֶר אֱלֹהִ֖ים יְהִ֣י א֑וֹר וַֽיְהִי־ 3
א֑וֹר׃ וַיַּ֧רְא אֱלֹהִ֛ים אֶת־הָא֖וֹר כִּי־ט֑וֹב וַיַּבְדֵּ֣ל אֱלֹהִ֔ים בֵּ֥ין 4
הָא֖וֹר וּבֵ֥ין הַחֹֽשֶׁךְ׃ וַיִּקְרָ֨א אֱלֹהִ֤ים ׀ לָאוֹר֙ י֔וֹם וְלַחֹ֖שֶׁךְ 5
קָ֣רָא לָ֑יְלָה וַֽיְהִי־עֶ֥רֶב וַֽיְהִי־בֹ֖קֶר י֥וֹם אֶחָֽד׃
פ
וַיֹּ֣אמֶר אֱלֹהִ֔ים יְהִ֥י רָקִ֖יעַ בְּת֣וֹךְ הַמָּ֑יִם וִיהִ֣י מַבְדִּ֔יל בֵּ֥ין 6
מַ֖יִם לָמָֽיִם׃ וַיַּ֣עַשׂ אֱלֹהִים֮ אֶת־הָרָקִיעַ֒ וַיַּבְדֵּ֗ל בֵּ֤ין הַמַּ֨יִם֙ 7
אֲשֶׁר֙ מִתַּ֣חַת לָרָקִ֔יעַ וּבֵ֣ין הַמַּ֔יִם אֲשֶׁ֖ר מֵעַ֣ל לָרָקִ֑יעַ וַֽיְהִי־
כֵֽן׃ וַיִּקְרָ֧א אֱלֹהִ֛ים לָֽרָקִ֖יעַ שָׁמָ֑יִם וַֽיְהִי־עֶ֥רֶב וַֽיְהִי־בֹ֖קֶר 8
י֥וֹם שֵׁנִֽי׃
פ
וַיֹּ֣אמֶר אֱלֹהִ֗ים יִקָּו֨וּ הַמַּ֜יִם מִתַּ֤חַת הַשָּׁמַ֨יִם֙ אֶל־מָק֣וֹם אֶחָ֔ד 9
וְתֵרָאֶ֖ה הַיַּבָּשָׁ֑ה וַֽיְהִי־כֵֽן׃ וַיִּקְרָ֨א אֱלֹהִ֤ים ׀ לַיַּבָּשָׁה֙ אֶ֔רֶץ 10
וּלְמִקְוֵ֥ה הַמַּ֖יִם קָרָ֣א יַמִּ֑ים וַיַּ֥רְא אֱלֹהִ֖ים כִּי־טֽוֹב׃ וַיֹּ֣אמֶר 11
אֱלֹהִ֗ים תַּֽדְשֵׁ֤א הָאָ֨רֶץ֙ דֶּ֔שֶׁא עֵ֚שֶׂב מַזְרִ֣יעַ זֶ֔רַע עֵ֣ץ פְּרִ֞י
עֹ֤שֶׂה פְּרִי֙ לְמִינ֔וֹ אֲשֶׁ֥ר זַרְעוֹ־ב֖וֹ עַל־הָאָ֑רֶץ וַֽיְהִי־כֵֽן׃
וַתּוֹצֵ֨א הָאָ֜רֶץ דֶּ֠שֶׁא עֵ֣שֶׂב מַזְרִ֤יעַ זֶ֨רַע֙ לְמִינֵ֔הוּ וְעֵ֧ץ עֹֽשֶׂה־ 12
פְּרִ֛י אֲשֶׁ֥ר זַרְעוֹ־ב֖וֹ לְמִינֵ֑הוּ וַיַּ֥רְא אֱלֹהִ֖ים כִּי־טֽוֹב׃ וַֽיְהִי־ 13
עֶ֥רֶב וַֽיְהִי־בֹ֖קֶר י֥וֹם שְׁלִישִֽׁי׃
פ
וַיֹּ֣אמֶר אֱלֹהִ֗ים יְהִ֤י מְאֹרֹת֙ בִּרְקִ֣יעַ הַשָּׁמַ֔יִם לְהַבְדִּ֕יל בֵּ֥ין 14
הַיּ֖וֹם וּבֵ֣ין הַלָּ֑יְלָה וְהָי֤וּ לְאֹתֹת֙ וּלְמ֣וֹעֲדִ֔ים וּלְיָמִ֖ים וְשָׁנִֽים׃
וְהָי֤וּ לִמְאוֹרֹת֙ בִּרְקִ֣יעַ הַשָּׁמַ֔יִם לְהָאִ֖יר עַל־הָאָ֑רֶץ וַֽיְהִי־ 15
כֵֽן׃

THE TORAH READING 23

The two Hebrew passages are the opening verses of בְּרֵאשִׁית (Bereshit), Genesis. The version below is in the hand-lettered style used throughout the *Sefer Torah*. It is the same text set by the Masoretes, where each word has vowels and a musical sign. The Masoretic text also has two small diamonds, one above the other, called a סוֹף פָּסוּק

בְּרֵאשִׁית בָּרָא אֱלֹהִים אֵת הַשָּׁמַיִם וְאֵת הָאָרֶץ
וְהָאָרֶץ הָיְתָה תֹהוּ וָבֹהוּ וְחֹשֶׁךְ עַל־פְּנֵי תְהוֹם וְרוּחַ
אֱלֹהִים מְרַחֶפֶת עַל־פְּנֵי הַמָּיִם וַיֹּאמֶר אֱלֹהִים יְהִי
אוֹר וַיְהִי־אוֹר וַיַּרְא אֱלֹהִים אֶת־הָאוֹר כִּי־טוֹב
וַיַּבְדֵּל אֱלֹהִים בֵּין הָאוֹר וּבֵין הַחֹשֶׁךְ וַיִּקְרָא
אֱלֹהִים לָאוֹר יוֹם וְלַחֹשֶׁךְ קָרָא לָיְלָה וַיְהִי־עֶרֶב
וַיְהִי־בֹקֶר יוֹם אֶחָד
וַיֹּאמֶר אֱלֹהִים יְהִי רָקִיעַ בְּתוֹךְ הַמָּיִם וִיהִי מַבְדִּיל
בֵּין מַיִם לָמָיִם וַיַּעַשׂ אֱלֹהִים אֶת־הָרָקִיעַ וַיַּבְדֵּל
בֵּין הַמַּיִם אֲשֶׁר מִתַּחַת לָרָקִיעַ וּבֵין הַמַּיִם אֲשֶׁר
מֵעַל לָרָקִיעַ וַיְהִי־כֵן וַיִּקְרָא אֱלֹהִים לָרָקִיעַ שָׁמָיִם
וַיְהִי־עֶרֶב וַיְהִי־בֹקֶר יוֹם שֵׁנִי
וַיֹּאמֶר אֱלֹהִים יִקָּווּ הַמַּיִם מִתַּחַת הַשָּׁמַיִם אֶל־
מָקוֹם אֶחָד וְתֵרָאֶה הַיַּבָּשָׁה וַיְהִי־כֵן וַיִּקְרָא אֱלֹהִים
לַיַּבָּשָׁה אֶרֶץ וּלְמִקְוֵה הַמַּיִם קָרָא יַמִּים וַיַּרְא
אֱלֹהִים כִּי־טוֹב וַיֹּאמֶר אֱלֹהִים תַּדְשֵׁא הָאָרֶץ
דֶּשֶׁא עֵשֶׂב מַזְרִיעַ זֶרַע עֵץ פְּרִי עֹשֶׂה פְּרִי לְמִינוֹ
אֲשֶׁר זַרְעוֹ־בוֹ עַל־הָאָרֶץ וַיְהִי־כֵן וַתּוֹצֵא הָאָרֶץ
דֶּשֶׁא עֵשֶׂב מַזְרִיעַ זֶרַע לְמִינֵהוּ וְעֵץ עֹשֶׂה פְּרִי
אֲשֶׁר זַרְעוֹ־בוֹ לְמִינֵהוּ וַיַּרְא אֱלֹהִים כִּי־טוֹב וַיְהִי־
עֶרֶב וַיְהִי־בֹקֶר יוֹם שְׁלִישִׁי
וַיֹּאמֶר אֱלֹהִים יְהִי מְאֹרֹת בִּרְקִיעַ הַשָּׁמַיִם לְהַבְדִּיל
בֵּין הַיּוֹם וּבֵין הַלָּיְלָה וְהָיוּ לְאֹתֹת וּלְמוֹעֲדִים וּלְיָמִים
וְשָׁנִים וְהָיוּ לִמְאוֹרֹת בִּרְקִיעַ הַשָּׁמַיִם לְהָאִיר עַל־
הָאָרֶץ וַיְהִי־כֵן

(sof pasuk), indicating that we have come to the end of a verse. There are, occasionally, other symbols which tell us about special vowel sounds. By providing all these signs, the Masoretes made it possible for us to read and chant the sacred writings as it was done in ancient times. In our religious schools, we use the vowelled and printed Masoretic text for the study of Bible; when we read the Torah portion at a synagogue service, it is done from the unvowelled *Sefer Torah* taken from the Ark.

The portion read each week is selected from lists of scriptural readings which were developed by rabbis in centuries past. In ancient Palestine, the rabbis divided up the *Chumash* into short weekly portions in such a way that it took three years to complete the reading of the Torah. The Babylonian rabbis, however, decided that it was more desirable to have the reading cycle over a period

THE TORAH READING

of one year. Thus, they made each week's portion much longer. Over the centuries, most Jews adopted the one-year Babylonian schedule of readings.

The list of scriptual readings for Reform congregations is found on pages 387-395 of the *Union Prayer Book*. There, the Torah readings are listed in the order in which they should be read, from בְּרֵאשִׁית *(Bereshit)*, In the Beginning, which is read on the Shabbat following *Simchat Torah*, to וְזֹאת הַבְּרָכָה *(Vezot Haberachah)*, And This Is the Blessing, which is the final *sidrah* read a year later.

After the reading of the weekly *sidrah* for which you were called to the pulpit, you will be privileged to say (or chant) the second set of *berachot*.

Blessed is the Lord our God, Ruler of the universe, who has given us a Torah of truth and implanted within us eternal life. Blessed is the Lord, Giver of Torah.	בָּרוּךְ אַתָּה יְיָ אֱלֹהֵינוּ, מֶלֶךְ הָעוֹלָם, אֲשֶׁר נָתַן לָנוּ תּוֹרַת אֱמֶת וְחַיֵּי עוֹלָם נָטַע בְּתוֹכֵנוּ. בָּרוּךְ אַתָּה יְיָ, נוֹתֵן הַתּוֹרָה.

The blessing before the Torah reading gave voice to the gratitude Jews in every age have felt for the gift of Torah at Sinai. Despite difficulties they faced in hostile surroundings over the years, they never, as a people, abandoned allegiance to it. When the reading of a portion is completed, the Jew who is called to the Torah recites this blessing, acknowledging that it is still the law of truth, still the guide to righteous living. As you prepare to say these *berachot* at your Bar/Bat Mitzvah service, you might try to think through how the ideas and laws of Torah relate to your own life.

THE HAFTARAH PORTION

We know that the custom of public Torah-readings evolved from the dramatic action of Ezra the Scribe. But scholars are not agreed as to how the practice of *haftarah* readings began. Some say that the Hebrew word *haftarah* really means "conclusion" or "dismissal," and that services in ancient times used to end with the reading of the *haftarah* portion.

A number of scholars, however, do not accept this view. They claim that *haftarah* readings were started during the reign of Antiochus IV, the Syrian-Greek ruler of the empire of which Judea was a part. About the year 175 B.C.E., this king embarked on a campaign to stamp out Judaism and force the Jews to become like the rest of his pagan subjects who worshipped him as one of their gods.

Among the first of the anti-Jewish decrees that Antiochus issued was an order forbidding our people to read or study the Torah. The Jews tried to get around this law during Torah-reading services, say these scholars, by reading from other sacred books. They selected passages from the Prophets or from the כְּתוּבִים (*Ketuvim*),

Writings, that had a special relationship to the *sidrah* that would have been read at the service. For instance, if the Torah portion dealt with Abraham, they would pick a selection from the Prophets that mentioned Abraham or that dealt with some event in his life.

After the Maccabees won religious freedom for the Jews, the decree of Antiochus was no longer in effect; the people were free to return to the customary Torah readings. This they were happy to do. But they had grown accustomed to the *haftarah* reading, say the scholars, and so they decided to continue that practice by adding it to the Torah service as a regular procedure.

There are scholars who give still another explanation. They maintain that the *haftarah* reading was introduced in order to combat the ideas of an ancient Hebrew sect, the Samaritans, who lived in Palestine. They believed that only the *Chumash*, which contained the word of God, was holy and therefore refused to accept any religious commandments or practices except those that were found in the Five Books of Moses. The Samaritans were only a small group. Their view was not held by most Jews who believed that all the books of the Bible were sacred. The reading of a *haftarah* portion confirmed that doctrine.

In actuality, we do not really know when and for what reason *haftarah* readings came to be included in our services, although we can say with some certainty that it is a very old practice. It is important, too, since it gives the congregation a chance to dip into other books of the Bible besides the *Chumash*.

The *haftarah* reading also has special *berachot* that precede it.

Blessed is the Lord our God, Ruler of the universe, who has chosen faithful prophets to speak words of truth.	בָּרוּךְ אַתָּה יְיָ אֱלֹהֵינוּ, מֶלֶךְ הָעוֹלָם, אֲשֶׁר בָּחַר בִּנְבִיאִים טוֹבִים וְרָצָה בְדִבְרֵיהֶם הַנֶּאֱמָרִים בֶּאֱמֶת.
Blessed is the Lord, for the revelation of Torah, for Moses His servant, and Israel His people, and for the prophets of truth and righteousness.	בָּרוּךְ אַתָּה יְיָ הַבּוֹחֵר בַּתּוֹרָה וּבְמֹשֶׁה עַבְדּוֹ וּבְיִשְׂרָאֵל עַמּוֹ וּבִנְבִיאֵי הָאֱמֶת וָצֶדֶק.

This set of *berachot* praises God for the prophets of old who, as spokesmen of God, spread His ideas of "truth and righteousness" among the people. The blessing suggests that the words about to be read (or chanted) were spoken by inspired men who reminded the Hebrews of the teachings of old which the Israelites, who had settled in Canaan, had begun to forget after a few centuries.

When you start to study your *haftarah* selection, you will learn that it contains an important message that is related to the *sidrah* of the week. Often, the *haftarah* selection has poetic elements that make the teachings of Torah come alive in dramatic ways. Perhaps your portion will help you see some of its teachings in a more personal way.

When you finish this reading, you will say (or chant) the *berachot* given below. These blessings, once more, will call attention to the sacredness of the words of the prophets. You will also be reminding the congregation that the God who gave us both the Torah and the prophets has also graced us with the Shabbat.

THE HAFTARAH PORTION

Blessed is the Lord our God, Ruler of the universe, Rock of all creation, Righteous One of all generations, the faithful God whose word is deed, whose every command is just and true.

בָּרוּךְ אַתָּה יְיָ אֱלֹהֵינוּ מֶלֶךְ הָעוֹלָם, צוּר כָּל הָעוֹלָמִים, צַדִּיק בְּכָל הַדּוֹרוֹת, הָאֵל הַנֶּאֱמָן, הָאוֹמֵר וְעוֹשֶׂה, הַמְדַבֵּר וּמְקַיֵּם שֶׁכָּל דְּבָרָיו אֱמֶת וָצֶדֶק.

For the Torah, for the privilege of worship, for the prophets, and for this Sabbath that You, O Lord our God, have given us for holiness and rest, for honor and glory, we thank and bless You. May Your name be blessed forever by every living being. Blessed is the Lord, for the Sabbath and its holiness.

עַל הַתּוֹרָה וְעַל הָעֲבוֹדָה וְעַל הַנְּבִיאִים וְעַל יוֹם הַשַּׁבָּת הַזֶּה שֶׁנָּתַתָּ לָּנוּ יְיָ אֱלֹהֵינוּ אֲנַחְנוּ מוֹדִים לָךְ וּמְבָרְכִים אוֹתָךְ. יִתְבָּרַךְ שִׁמְךָ בְּפִי כָּל חַי תָּמִיד לְעוֹלָם וָעֶד. בָּרוּךְ אַתָּה יְיָ מְקַדֵּשׁ הַשַּׁבָּת.

Now, the Scripture-reading part of the service comes to a close. At this point, many congregations provide an opportunity for the Bar/Bat Mitzvah to make a personal statement, generally one of thanks and appreciation for all those who have helped him or her to this time of life, and to express his or her own thoughts on the meaning of the ceremony. If this is customary in your congregation, you will be asked to write this statement which could be in the form of a prayer or short speech.

Your congregation may also provide for either one or both of your parents to give a blessing of their own.

The Torah scroll is now ready to be returned to the Ark. It is lifted up by the rabbi and brought to the Ark. With the congregation standing, some final passages are recited, poetically summarizing the deep respect of the people Israel for the Torah:

The Torah of the Lord is perfect, reviving the soul.	תּוֹרַת יְיָ תְּמִימָה, מְשִׁיבַת נָפֶשׁ.
The teaching of the Lord is sure, making wise the simple.	עֵדוּת יְיָ נֶאֱמָנָה, מַחְכִּימַת פֶּתִי.
The precepts of the Lord are right, delighting the mind.	פִּקּוּדֵי יְיָ יְשָׁרִים, מְשַׂמְּחֵי לֵב.
The mitzvah of the Lord is clear, giving light to the eyes.	מִצְוַת יְיָ בָּרָא, מְאִירַת עֵינָיִם.
The word of the Lord is pure, enduring forever.	יִרְאַת יְיָ טְהוֹרָה, עוֹמֶדֶת לָעַד.
The judgments of the Lord are true, and altogether just.	מִשְׁפְּטֵי יְיָ אֱמֶת. צָדְקוּ יַחְדָּו.
Behold, a good doctrine has been given you, My Torah. Do not forsake it.	כִּי לֶקַח טוֹב נָתַתִּי לָכֶם תּוֹרָתִי אַל תַּעֲזוֹבוּ.

After the ritual of returning the Torah to the Ark, the rabbi will ask you to stand with him or her on the *bimah*. He or she will deliver a sermonette directed to you personally, in which some part of the *sidrah* or *haftarah* portion will be related to your life, interests, and concerns. At the end of the talk, the rabbi will confer a special blessing on you.

In most congregations, the Sisterhood or Brotherhood (or both) will present a gift to you; then the rabbi will begin the concluding portion of the worship service. You will probably feel quite relieved when it ends but, in all likelihood, you will also feel a kind of thrill inside you for Bar/Bat Mitzvah is a really exciting experience. You will truly be ready to celebrate with your friends and family.

THE FAMILY CELEBRATES BAR/BAT MITZVAH

In addition to your own participation in the service, other members of your family may receive honors at the time of your celebration. In some congregations the mother of the Bar/Bat Mitzvah blesses the Shabbat lights and the father chants the קדוּשׁ *(Kiddush)*, blessing over wine, at the עֶרֶב שַׁבָּת *(Erev Shabbat)*, Sabbath eve, service the night before. During the Bar/Bat Mitzvah service itself, close members of your family, such as your parents and grandparents, may be honored with an *aliyah* or by being asked to sit on the pulpit, or to help with the dressing of the Torah. In whatever manner the congregation conducts its services, your family will, in some way, be involved in it.

In Judaism, the family has always been regarded as a sort of small congregation. Throughout the year a family celebrates religious holidays and ceremonies in the home. On Friday nights, it is part of our tradition to say blessings over the Shabbat candles at home and to recite the *Kiddush* and blessings connected with the Shabbat meal.

At Pesach, the head of the house conducts a סֵדֶר, Seder, which is really a worship service. At Chanukah, candles are blessed and lit and a variety of holiday songs are sung. A בְּרִית (berit), the covenant of circumcision, and a wedding are examples of other religious practices that may be performed and celebrated in the home.

It is not at all surprising, therefore, that the family is very much involved in the celebration of the Bar/Bat Mitzvah. In fact, the observance cannot really take place unless the parents (or guardians) of the child participate actively in preparations for it, which begin long before the event. The parents, after all, must first make the decision to enroll the child in a religious school. By their financial support, the parents enable temples to provide the kind of religious education and training that makes the beliefs and practices of our faith meaningful to modern children.

There is every reason for parents and grandparents to experience נַחַת (nachat), pleasure, when a member of their family becomes Bar/Bat Mitzvah. Aside from the personal pride they feel, there is also a sense of satisfaction in seeing that the honored traditions of our people are being kept alive.

To the family, the Bar/Bat Mitzvah day is, therefore, a special *simchah*. It is natural for them to have a festive meal and to invite friends and relatives to share their joy with them. There has been a tendency, however, for some families, in the past and present, to make very elaborate celebrations. And, just as people of the Cracow Jewish community did in 1595, many Jews today are questioning whether the celebration calls for such lavish festivities. In the eyes of the critics, the party or reception should mark a memorable and meaningful step in religious growth. They urge people, therefore, to use moderation so that the spiritual significance of the event is not lost.

Some families have taken this to heart and have revived the Jewish custom of sharing a personal *simchah* with the larger Jewish community. With the full participation of the prospective Bar/Bat Mitzvah, they decide to make contributions in honor of the boy or girl to various educational and charitable funds sponsored by the family or temple. If something like this is done by your family, you will have a chance to consider the kind of service or institution you would like to support. This will add to your joy, knowing that your coming of age was a source of help in strengthening various organizations which devote themselves to caring for those in need and for the well-being of the Jewish community.

In any case, your Bar/Bat Mitzvah is an occasion for celebrating. No doubt, both the religious and social aspects will remain in your memory for a long time. But what will make your preparations for the Shabbat service truly meaningful depends on how well you put together what you studied and thought through in the months before it. For then you will know better what you prize in your religion and the traditions of your people, and you will better understand yourself as a Jew. In addition, you will be able to participate more knowledgeably in future temple services, whether as a member of a congregation or as one who has been called to the *bimah* in honor of the Torah.

What Are You When You Are Bar/Bat Mitzvah?

As you embark on the concentrated study of material for your Bar/Bat Mitzvah, it would be well to consider, once again, what the whole ceremony really means.

As we said earlier, it is only your religious status that changes, and that is not immediately felt or seen in concrete forms. It does mean that you become eligible for an *aliyah*, that you can read or chant the *Kiddush* at a worship service, and that you can be counted for a *minyan*. But there may be no real "evidence" to show that anything special has happened. You seem to be the same boy or girl as before, faced with the same tasks at school, the same chores at home, and involved in the same hobbies, games, and interests.

And, yet, you are really not the same; from that moment on, a new relationship exists between you and the *mitzvot* of our faith. According to the Jewish religious tradition, the Bar/Bat Mitzvah is supposed to assume responsibility for carrying out the commandments of Judaism. In other words, our tradition calls upon you to become thoroughly acquainted with the teachings of Judaism, for you are expected to use them as guides for your everyday life.

It is obvious, then, that if you accept Bar/Bat Mitzvah as an important religious experience, you must also accept the need for further and deeper study about your religion and its traditions. The celebration is not an end but rather a beginning, the start of more serious study of the philosophical and ethical ideas of Judaism. This does not mean merely to gather more information about our faith and people. It means coming to understand all these matters in relation to your own life. Jews have done this in every generation, pondering what meaning the prophetic message, from Moses and Amos onward, had for their own day.

That is one of the reasons why Reform Judaism has placed so much emphasis upon Confirmation, for this religious step upward comes after a person has had a few more years of organized study at a higher level of religious and historical understanding. At Confirmation, therefore, you will be much closer than you are now to an appreciation of the goals and aims of Judaism.

This should be noted: At no time in our long history have Jews looked upon our religion as something that one studies only during one's childhood. Schools in ancient Palestine and the famous academies of Sura and Pumbedita in Babylonia, as well as those in medieval Spain, were attended by adults, not children. Also, in the time of your grandparents and great-grandparents, it was adults who used to meet with the rabbi or some other scholar on Saturday afternoons (or on other days of the week) to study. Jews have always taken seriously the idea that: "This book of the law shall not depart out of your mouth, but you shall meditate therein day and night, that you may observe to do according to all that is written therein." (Joshua 1:8)

There is an old saying, in Mishnah Pe'ah 1:1, that: תַּלְמוּד תּוֹרָה כְּנֶגֶד כֻּלָּם (Talmud Torah keneged kulam), "The study of Torah is greater than all else." That is why our synagogues devote so much time to organizing high school classes in Hebrew and general religious studies, study programs for temple youth groups, and adult education programs, so that people of all ages may continue to study and learn about our religion and way of life.

As a Bar/Bat Mitvah student, you are part of this great tradition. Although you are only at the start of the mature study of Judaism, you are doing something that will give you, your family, and friends much pleasure. It will be this way with the many joyous occasions that the future holds in store for you: The more you study, the happier your participation in Jewish life will be.

מַזָּל טוֹב (Mazal tov), Congratulations and good luck! May your coming of age bring much joy to you and to your family and friends!

Now you can look forward to your next Jewish milestone, your Confirmation. This will be a *coming-of-age* of another kind.

GLOSSARY

The Hebrew words are listed below in the order in which they appear in the text.

Bar/Bat Mitzvah — "Son/Daughter בַּר/בַּת מִצְוָה
of the Commandment."   1
Bimah — Pulpit.   1 בִּימָה
Simchat Torah — שִׂמְחַת תּוֹרָה
Rejoicing of the Torah.   1
Devarim — Deuteronomy.   1 דְּבָרִים
Chumash — The Pentateuch; חוּמָשׁ
the Five Books of Moses.   1-2
Bereshit — Genesis; In the Beginning.   2, 23 בְּרֵאשִׁית
Aliyah — "Going up" to read עֲלִיָה
from the Torah.   2
Haftarah — A selected reading הַפְטָרָה
from the Prophets
read after the Torah portion.   3
Minyan — Quorum (ten adult male Jews, מִנְיָן
the minimum for congregational prayer).   3
Berachot — Blessings.   4 בְּרָכוֹת
Sidrah — Torah portion of the week.   4 סִדְרָה
Berit Milah — Circumcision.   5 בְּרִית מִילָה
Tanach — The Hebrew Bible.   5 תַּנַ״ךְ
Pirke Avot — Sayings of the Fathers.   6 פִּרְקֵי אָבוֹת
Ben shelosh-esreh lamitzvot — בֶּן שְׁלֹשׁ־עֶשְׂרֵה לַמִצְווֹת
Thirteen [is the age] for [the
fulfillment of] the commandments.   6

Baruch shepetarani me'onsho shel zeh — Blessed be He who has freed me from the [religious] responsibility for this child.	6	בָּרוּךְ שֶׁפְּטָרַנִי מֵעָנְשׁוֹ שֶׁל זֶה
Shabbat — Sabbath.	7	שַׁבָּת
Talit — Prayer shawl.	7	טַלִית
Tefilin — Phylacteries (two black leather boxes fastened to leather straps, containing four portions from the Torah).	7	תְּפִילִין
Simchah — A joyful occasion.	7	שִׂמְחָה
Mechitzah — Partition.	10	מְחִיצָה
Kohanim — Temple priests.	14	כֹּהֲנִים
Rosh Hashanah — The New Year.	15	רֹאשׁ הַשָּׁנָה
Sefer Torah — Scroll of the Torah.	17	סֵפֶר תּוֹרָה
Neviim — Prophets.	17	נְבִיאִים
Aron Hakodesh — The Holy Ark.	18	אָרוֹן הַקֹּדֶשׁ
Naaseh Venishma — We will do and obey.	18	נַעֲשֶׂה וְנִשְׁמַע
Nekudot — Vowel points.	20	נְקוּדוֹת
Neginot — Signs for the chant.	20	נְגִינוֹת
Mitah — Bed.	21	מִטָה
Mateh — Stick.	21	מַטֶה
Matah — Down.	21	מַטָה
Muteh — Injustice.	21	מֻטֶה
Mutah — Outspreading.	21	מֻטָה
Sof pasuk — End of verse (special cantillation sign).	24	סוֹף פָּסוּק

GLOSSARY

Vezot Haberachah —
 And This Is the Blessing. 25 וְזֹאת הַבְּרָכָה
Ketuvim — Writings. 27 כְּתוּבִים
Kiddush — Blessing over wine. 31 קִדּוּשׁ
Erev Shabbat — Sabbath eve. 31 עֶרֶב שַׁבָּת
Seder — The Passover ceremony. 32 סֵדֶר
Nachat — Pleasure. 32 נַחַת
*Talmud Torah Keneged
 Kulam* — The study of Torah
 is greater than all else. 36 תַּלְמוּד תּוֹרָה כְּנֶגֶד כֻּלָּם
Mazal tov — Congratulations
 and good luck. 36 מַזָּל טוֹב

Commission on Jewish Education
of the
Union of American Hebrew Congregations
and the
Central Conference of American Rabbis
as of 1977

Chairman
Martin S. Rosenberg

Honorary Chairman
Solomon B. Freehof

Dr. Dorothy G. Axelroth
Morton A. Bauman
Herbert M. Baumgard
Alan D. Bennett
Leo Bergman
Morrison David Bial
Eric Feldheim
Harvey J. Fields
Leon C. Fram

Stuart Gertman
Roland B. Gittelsohn
David S. Hachen
Jack Horowitz
Bernard Kligfeld
Ronald Kronish
Mrs. David M. Levitt
Louis Lister
Stanley Meisels
Sally Priesand

Mrs. Cecil B. Rudnick
Dr. Lenore Sandel
Frederick C. Schwartz
Sylvan D. Schwartzman
L. William Spear
Marvin S. Walts
Heinz Warschauer
Martin Weiner
Sue Weiskopf

Ex Officio
Matthew Ross
Alexander M. Schindler

William C. Cutter
Joseph B. Glaser
Arthur J. Lelyveld

Sadie Segal
Dr. Paul Steinberg
Bernard M. Zlotowitz

Abraham Segal

Union Education Series
Edited by
Daniel B. Syme, *Director of Education*
Steven M. Reuben, *Assistant Director*

Director of Publications
Ralph Davis

Editor of Keeping Posted
Edith Samuel